THE STORY OF THE WORLD CUP

RICHARD BRASSEY

Orion
Children's Books

First published in Great Britain in 2014
by Orion Children's Books
a division of the Orion Publishing Group Ltd
Orion House, 5 Upper St Martin's Lane, London WC2H 9EA
An Hachette UK company

10 9 8 7 6 5 4 3 2 1

Text and illustrations copyright © Richard Brassey 2014

The right of Richard Brassey to be identified as the author
and illustrator of this work has been asserted.

FIFA WORLD CUP is a registered trademark of Fédération Internationale de Football Association (FIFA)
WORLD CUP is a registered trademark of Fédération Internationale de Football Association (FIFA)
Jules Rimet is a registered trademark of Fédération Internationale de Football Association (FIFA)
FIFA is a registered trademark of Fédération Internationale de Football Association (FIFA)
BRAZIL 2014 is a registered trademark of Fédération Internationale de Football Association (FIFA)

A catalogue record for this book is available from the British Library

The Orion Publishing Group's policy is to use papers that are natural, renewable and recyclable
products and made from wood grown in sustainable forests. The logging and manufacturing
processes are expected to conform to the environmental regulations of the country of origin.

Printed in Singapore

ISBN 978 1 4440 0946 0

www.orionbooks.co.uk

THE FIFA WORLD CUP TROPHY

Every four years the name of the country that wins the World Cup is engraved on the bottom of the trophy. But after 2038 there'll be no room for any more. What will FIFA do? Maybe they'll make a new cup. It wouldn't be the first time (see page 17).

Soccer is easily the most popular type of football in the world. In most of the two hundred countries where it is played, it's known simply as 'football' even though players of other football games may find this annoying.

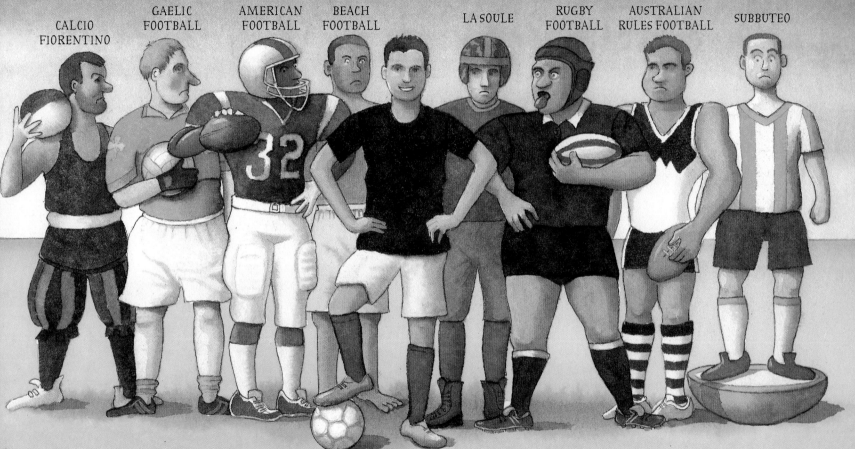

CALCIO FIORENTINO — GAELIC FOOTBALL — AMERICAN FOOTBALL — BEACH FOOTBALL — LA SOULE — RUGBY FOOTBALL — AUSTRALIAN RULES FOOTBALL — SUBBUTEO

And since the soccer World Cup is the most popular international sporting event of any kind – bigger even than the Olympics – it's often known simply as 'the World Cup'.

The ancient Greeks and Romans played several types of football. Nobody knows much about them except that a lot of people got hurt while playing.

A soccer-like game called Cuju – meaning *kick the ball* – was popular in ancient China. It was usually played with a leather ball – often full of feathers – and with goal posts made from bamboo.

In medieval Europe, mob football was so popular and dangerous that several kings banned it. There don't seem to have been any rules about where it was played, the size of the teams, or even how the players got the ball to the goal!

HOW SOCCER GOT ITS NAME

So a forward is offside unless there are four defenders between him and the goal?

No, that should only be three!

The rules of the modern game were first written down by the English Football Association in 1863 and it was given the grand title of 'Association Football'. People found this a bit of a mouthful and soon shortened 'association' to 'soccer'.

This trophy in the Scottish Football Museum proves that in 1888 Renton FC were 'Champions of the United Kingdom and the World'!

The first ever championship between teams from different countries was played in 1888 when the Scottish league winners, Renton Football Club, beat English champions, West Bromwich Albion. In Scotland they'll tell you this was the first World Cup. Renton FC ceased to exist in 1922 but you can still see the cup they won in the Scottish Football Museum.

In England they'll speak of another long-vanished team named Upton Park who won gold at the 1900 Olympics – or perhaps of West Auckland FC who won an international tournament in Italy in 1909. In Switzerland they'll say the first champions were Servette FC in 1908. But these were club matches. None were the World Cup between national teams as we know it today.

STOLEN CUP!

In 1994 the international trophy won by West Auckland eighty-five years earlier was stolen. All you can see today is a replica.

THE FIRST OFFICIAL WORLD CUP

FIFA stands for *Fédération Internationale de Football Association*, which is French for *International Federation of Association Football*. It was founded in 1904 and organised a series of amateur football tournaments as part of the Olympics, but it was not until Jules Rimet became president that they decided to hold their own international tournament open to national teams of professional players. The first true World Cup was held in Uruguay in 1930. Jules carried the famous trophy – which was named after him – all the way from France to South America in his bag.

URUGUAY 1930

Before the days of passenger planes, it took at least a fortnight to sail from Europe to Uruguay. Only four European teams made it – Belgium, France, Yugoslavia and Romania. They arrived to find fog and rain and bumpy pitches. The main stadium was only just finished in time for the final in which Uruguay beat Argentina 4-2 to become first ever official World Cup Champions.

ITALY 1934

The host country again won the second World Cup when Italy triumphed four years later in Rome. They won again in 1938 and held the cup while the tournament was suspended through World War Two. They were expected to win again in 1950 but, just before the competition, tragedy struck. Turin had an especially talented team at that time known as *Il Grande Torino*. Ten of the players were also in the national team. But, tragically, all were killed when their plane crashed into Superga Hill, near Turin, on their way home from a match.

All through World War Two, Italian vice-president of FIFA, Dr Ottorino Barassi, kept the Jules Rimet trophy safely hidden in a shoebox under his bed.

BRAZIL 1950

Instead of Italy, Uruguay once again became world champions, beating Brazil in the 1950 final.

1950 saw England compete for the first time. When they were defeated 1-0 in the group stage by a USA team of part-timers, the UK newspapers couldn't believe such a score. They assumed it was a misprint and at first reported that England had won 10-0.

ALF RAMSEY
Playing in defence in that unfortunate match was a young man named Alf Ramsey, who went on to become the England manager and lead them to victory in 1966.

CHAMPION OF CHAMPIONS

GREATEST PLAYER EVER

Brazil have competed in every World Cup. In the 1950 final they lost at home to Uruguay in the new Maracanã Stadium, also host to the 2014 final. They didn't first win the trophy until 1958, but since then they have been champions four more times – more than any other nation.

Pelé first appeared for Brazil, aged seventeen, in the 1958 Sweden World Cup. The only player ever to be part of three world champion squads, he is said by many to be the greatest of all time.

WORLD CUP CHAMPIONS

Only eight countries can boast of winning the World Cup. Five of them have won it more than once.

Five times:

Brazil: 1958, 1962, 1970, 1994, 2002

Four times:

Italy: 1934, 1938, 1982, 2006

Three times:

Germany: 1954, 1974, 1990

Two times:

Uruguay: 1930, 1950
Argentina: 1978, 1986

Once:

England: 1966
France: 1998
Spain: 2010

LUXEMBOURG'S WORLD CUP RECORD

Only one team has competed in every World Cup qualifying round yet never qualified. They've lost all but a couple of matches and nearly always come bottom of their group. You can't accuse them of not trying, but then the population of tiny Luxembourg is four hundred times smaller than that of mighty Brazil.

THE GOLDEN BOOT

After every World Cup the Golden Boot Award goes to the player who has scored the most goals in that tournament. The players who have scored the most World Cup goals during their careers are:

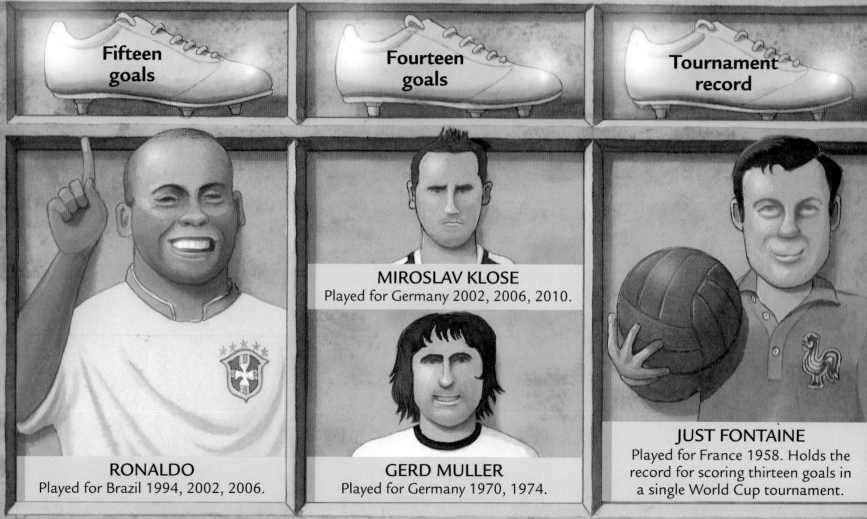

Fifteen goals

Fourteen goals

Tournament record

MIROSLAV KLOSE
Played for Germany 2002, 2006, 2010.

RONALDO
Played for Brazil 1994, 2002, 2006.

GERD MULLER
Played for Germany 1970, 1974.

JUST FONTAINE
Played for France 1958. Holds the record for scoring thirteen goals in a single World Cup tournament.

THE OLDEST PLAYER

ROGER MILLA

When the President of Cameroon begged him to come out of retirement to play in USA 1994, Roger became the oldest World Cup player ever at 42. He also became the oldest goalscorer, celebrating with his trademark goal dance.

GOAL OF THE CENTURY

In 1986, Argentina versus England, Diego Maradona scored what is generally considered the greatest World Cup goal ever. He dashed from well within his own half, past four England players and round the goalkeeper to score!

CHILE 1962

As England battled champions Brazil in 1962, a small black dog ran onto the pitch and danced rings round Brazil's finest until England striker, Jimmy Greaves, dropped on all fours and managed to scoop him up. The excitement was too much. The pooch did a wee all down his shirt.

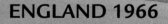

ENGLAND 1966

It was a proud moment at Wembley in 1966 when Queen Elizabeth II presented the trophy to home team, England. But the fact that there was a trophy to present at all was down to a small doggy hero named Pickles . . .

PICKLES and the STOLEN CUP

A few months earlier, the trophy had been stolen from an exhibition in London while the security guards took a tea break.

Where's the cup?

I don't have it.

A ransom was paid. The police arrested the man who collected it but he didn't have the trophy. All seemed lost.

A few evenings later, Pickles was out for a walk near his home when he sniffed out a package under a holly bush. His owner unwrapped it and inside was the Jules Rimet trophy!

Pickles became front page news. He was even given a medal.

STOLEN AGAIN!

After Brazil won the cup for the third time in 1970 they got to keep the Jules Rimet. FIFA had to make a new trophy. In 1983 a hooded man broke into Soccer HQ in Rio, tied up the night watchman and stole the Jules Rimet. It was never seen again.

In 1966, referee Ken Aston had a brainwave while sitting in his car at a traffic light. His red and yellow card system was first used during Mexico 1970.

Diabolical!

Ludicrous!

Farcical!

The ref is the one who should be given a yellow card

Russian referee Valentin Ivanov handed out sixteen yellow and four red cards during the Germany 2006 second-round match between Portugal and Holland – the most ever in a World Cup match. However, many thought Valentin had been too enthusiastic and not all the cards had been deserved.

INFAMOUS FOULS

There have been many fouls in World Cup history. These are three of the most infamous which the ref failed to spot, although they were seen by millions of television viewers:

FOUL OF THE CENTURY

In 1982, German goalkeeper, Toni Schumacher, rushed French striker, Patrick Battiston, and knocked out two of his teeth.

THE HAND OF GOD

In 1986, Argentina captain, Diego Maradona, sneakily used his hand to punch the ball into the net of England goalkeeper, Peter Shilton. Moments after that goal was allowed, he raced through the stupefied England defence to score the Goal of the Century (see page 15).

THE HAND OF HENRY

In a 2010 qualifier between France and Ireland, Thierry Henry touched the ball twice while setting up the winning goal.

HIGHEST WORLD CUP SCORE EVER

American Samoa had not had a national team very long when Australia beat them in a 2001 qualifier. The ball hardly left the back of the Samoan net . . . Final score 31-0!

In 2002, on the same day as the official World Cup final in Japan, a friendly was played high in the Himalayan kingdom of Bhutan. Bhutan, then second bottom of the FIFA World Rankings, beat the Caribbean island nation of Montserrat, then bottom. The score was 4-0.

20

WORLD CUP COIFFURES

From Sir Bobby Charlton's comb-over, to Carlos Valderrama's haystack, to Roberto Baggio's magic ponytail, many World Cup players have sported interesting hairstyles.

BOBBY CHARLTON
England

PAUL BREITNER
Germany

CHRIS WADDLE
England

DAVID BECKHAM
England

CARLOS VALDERRAMA
Colombia

TARIBO WEST
Nigeria

ABEL XAVIER
Portugal

ROBERTO BAGGIO
Italy

RONALDO
Brazil

In 1998, the whole Romanian squad went blond for luck – except the keeper who was bald. It wasn't very lucky though. They failed to win a match after that.

The World Cup has been held in North and South America, Europe, Asia and Africa.

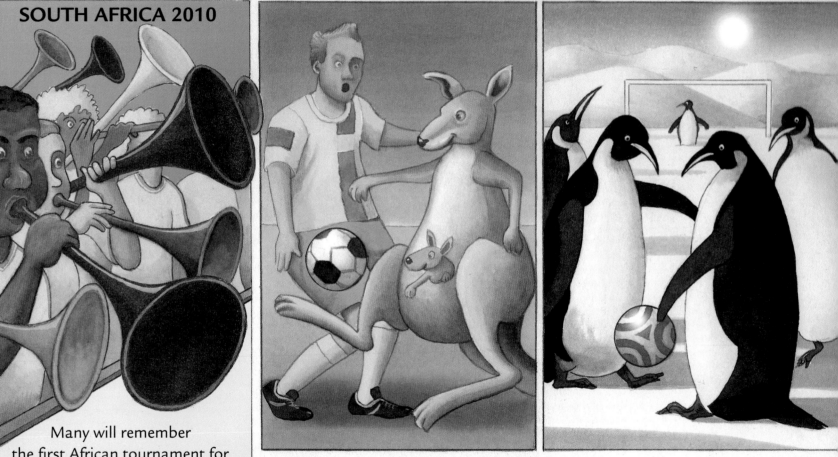

SOUTH AFRICA 2010

Many will remember the first African tournament for the constant sound of vuvuzela horns which spectators blew throughout every game.

The only continents where the World Cup has not yet been held are Oceania, which includes Australia and the Pacific Islands, and Antarctica. As far as we know there are no football teams in Antarctica!

BRAZIL 2014

Scotland's claim to the first World Cup may be shaky, but there's no denying a Scot, named Thomas Donohue, really started something when he organised the first ever soccer match in Rio de Janeiro in 1894. Brazilians are soccer mad. They play everywhere . . . on streets, on beaches, in gyms. Traffic stops, banks close, everything halts when the national team plays. 2014 is the second final Rio has hosted.

GOAL LINE TECHNOLOGY

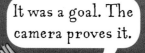

FIFA decided that cameras would be introduced in 2014 to help decide if the ball has crossed the goal line or not. This has upset some fans who think the best part of soccer is arguing about the referee's mistakes!

The World Cup is hosted by a different country every four years

Host Country	Winner	Final Stadium
1930 Uruguay	Uruguay	Estadio Centenario, Montevideo
1934 Italy	Italy	Stadio Nazionale, Rome
1938 France	Italy	Stade Olympique, Paris
1950 Brazil	Uruguay	Estadio do Maracanã, Rio de Janeiro
1954 Switzerland	West Germany	Wankdorf Stadium, Bern
1958 Sweden	Brazil	Råsunda Fotbollstadion, Stockholm
1962 Chile	Brazil	Estadio Nacional, Santiago
1966 England	England	Wembley Stadium, London
1970 Mexico	Brazil	Estadio Azteca, Mexico City
1974 West Germany	West Germany	Olympiastadion, Munich
1978 Argentina	Argentina	Estadio Monumental, Buenos Aires
1982 Spain	Italy	Estadio Santiago Bernabéu, Madrid
1986 Mexico	Argentina	Estadio Azteca, Mexico City
1990 Italy	West Germany	Stadio Olimpico, Rome
1994 USA	Brazil	Rose Bowl, Pasadena
1998 France	France	Stade de France, Paris
2002 South Korea/Japan	Brazil	Nissan Stadium, Yokohama
2006 Germany	Italy	Olympic Stadium, Berlin
2010 South Africa	Spain	Soccer City, Soweto
2014 Brazil		Estadio do Maracanã, Rio de Janeiro
2018 Russia		Luzhniki Stadium, Moscow
2022 Qatar		Lusail Iconic Stadium, Lusail